John Blaksley

Footprints of the lion and other stories of travel

John Blaksley

Footprints of the lion and other stories of travel

ISBN/EAN: 9783337206222

Printed in Europe, USA, Canada, Australia, Japan

Cover: Foto ©Andreas Hilbeck / pixelio.de

More available books at **www.hansebooks.com**

FOOTPRINTS OF THE LION

AND OTHER

STORIES OF TRAVEL.

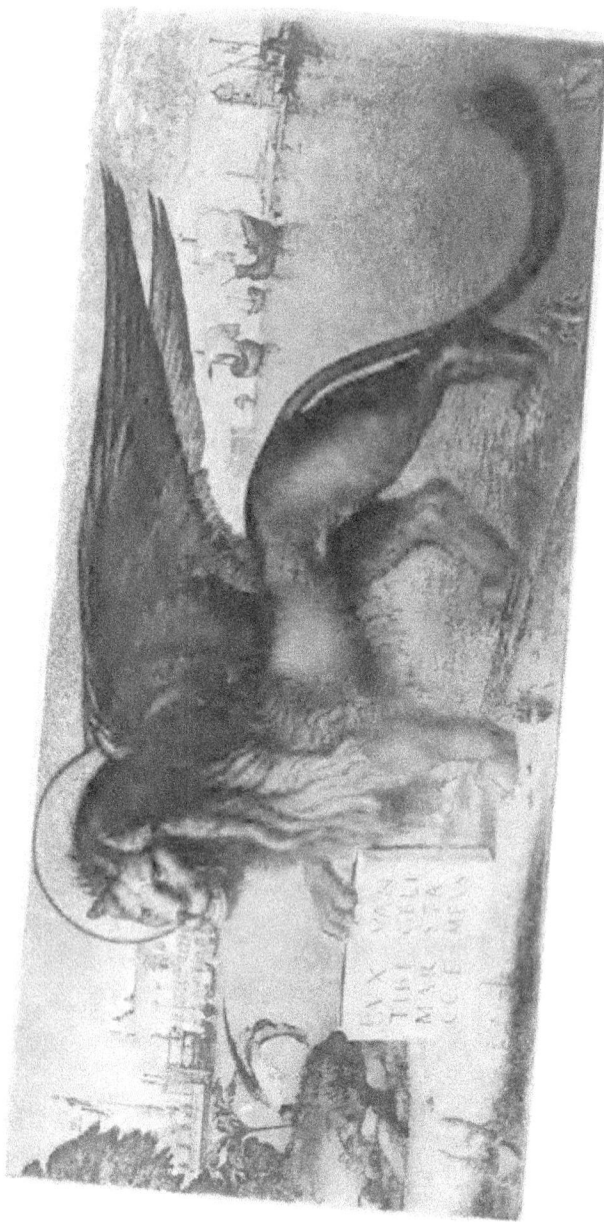

FOOTPRINTS OF THE LION

AND OTHER

STORIES OF TRAVEL.

BY

MAJOR-GENERAL J. BLAKSLEY.

With Frontispiece and **Thirty-two** *Illustrations from Photographs, &c.*

LONDON:
W. H. ALLEN & CO., LIMITED,
13, WATERLOO PLACE, S.W.
1896.

MALCOMSON AND CO., LIMITED,
PRINTERS,
LONDON AND REDHILL.

DEDICATED,

BY PERMISSION,

TO MY KIND FRIEND AND KINDLIEST CRITIC,

Mrs. De Vere Brook

(UNA SHERIDAN),

AS A SLIGHT TRIBUTE OF THE HIGHEST ADMIRATION

FOR THE LOVE-COMPELLING BEAUTY, AND HER SWEET SOCIETY,

AND IN ANTICIPATION OF ONE OF HER PRETTY SMILES OF APPROVAL,

THE VERY THOUGHT OF WHICH ALONE IS INSPIRATION,

AND THE HOPE FOR WHICH ALONE HAS BROUGHT TO LIGHT

THESE STORIES.

CONTENTS.

		PAGE
I.	FOOTPRINTS OF THE LION ...	1
II.	EASTWARDS	35
III.	THE EVIL EYE; OR, THE COLONEL IN QUEST OF HIS REGIMENT	57
IV.	THE EXPECTED BUDDHA; OR, THE ROYAL TWINS	103

LIST OF ILLUSTRATIONS.

The Lion of St. Mark's	*Frontispiece*	
Sebenico	To face page	2
The River Ombla	,, ,,	4
Curzola	,, ,,	6
Kerka Falls	,, ,,	8
Zara	,, ,,	10
The Walls of Diocletian's Palace	,, ,,	12
The Campanile at Spalăto	,, ,,	14
Porta Aurea	,, ,,	16
Spalăto	,, ,,	18
The Peristyleum at Salona	,, ,,	20
The Amphitheatre at Salona	,, ,,	22
Entrance to the Mausoleum, Spalăto	,, ,,	24
Ragusa	,, ,,	26
Cattăro	,, ,,	28
La Croma	,, ,,	30
Lussin Grande	,, ,,	32
La Croma	,, ,,	34
Lucknow	,, ,,	44
The Dhul Canal, Kashmir	,, ,,	48
The Modern Nourmahal	,, ,,	50
Nynee Tal	,, ,,	52
The Pindari Glacier	,, ,,	55
The Ear of Dionysius	,, ,,	74
Messina	,, ,,	80
Bastia	,, ,,	88
Nôtre Dame de la Garde	,, ,,	92
Singapore	,, ,,	100
Bangkok	,, ,,	106
A Canal at Bangkok	,, ,,	108
Interior of Royal Temple	,, ,,	110
Wat Chang	,, ,,	112
Entrance to Wat Chang	,, ,,	114

I.
FOOTPRINTS OF THE LION.

SEBENICO. [*To face page 2.*

FOOTPRINTS OF THE LION.

CHAPTER I.

NOT the overrated, common, desert or jungle wallah, but the proud old Lion of San Marco, with his dextral uplift, and his "*Pax tibi Marce, Evangelista meus.*" Are you a lover of Venice, and her history? Would you roam in fields and pastures new? Then, with your two gladstone-bags, start early in April for a cruise in the Eastern Adriatic. It is *via* Trieste that you proceed to visit these delightful old-world places, these possessions of Old Venice when she was Queen of the Sea.

There are many whose idea of travelling is exemplified by an arrow when shot from a bow,—its main object is to gain its destination, and everything *en route*, no matter how interesting, is to be ignored. Now, we all know that every road leads to Rome, and similarly, there are many ways of getting to Trieste. We will not hurry on the good old *arrow* principle, but leave that for *flighty* people, who had much better start by steamer from London Bridge and go direct somewhere—*anywhere*, and stay there.

If you are going from England, as pleasant a way as any is this:—Leave Victoria at 11 a.m., and arrive at Brussels for dinner; similarly next day to Luxembourg; next Carlsruhe; next Munich for three days,

THE RIVER OMBLA.

and let Sunday be one of them; next Botzen; next Verona; and then Venice the ex-Queen. The Austrian Lloyd steamers are plentiful from Trieste; they are scrupulously clean and well appointed, and are the "best hotels in the Adriatic"; the officers are educated gentlemen whom it is a pleasure to know; they and the stewards all talk Italian, as well as German; of course, as the whole of Dalmatia belongs to Austria, and Herzegovina and Bosnia are under her protection, most of the travellers in these parts are Austrian, and German is the language most heard on *board*. In securing your berth, Oh, gentle *viaggiatore!* beware of the "*Allgemeine cabine*,"—they hold eight, and ventilation seems objected to, especially at night; therefore, unless you are impervious to all that is malodorous, and especially favoured by the good god Somnus, beware!

a ponderous, apoplectic, beer-imbibing *Tedesco* on his back recumbent, his mouth wide open to the noxious air, uttering sounds, stertorous, loud, and ungodly enough to awake the tenantry of a *Campo Santo*, will not induce "nature's sweet restorer"; and, as you lie contemplating him by the never-extinguished electric glare, in respectful wonderment, you do not regard him as "a thing of beauty," although doubtless "a joy for ever" to his "*liebe Frau,*" whom he has most carefully left at home.

The writer had one night of this, but it was well-nigh forgotten in the beautiful freshness of the early morn, coasting along the picturesque shore of Ischia, with the snowy peaks of the Julian Alps as a background; Pirano, Parenzo were passed, and Rovigno attracted much attention,—hark! what sweet sounds are these?

CURZOLA.

[*To face page 6.*

"Ach! Gott! es ist schön,—— "

"Yaw!"

"Es ist wunderschön!"

"Und gross!"

"Yaw!"

Chorus of "Yaw! Yaw!"

The good ship *Metkovich* is bound for Pola, however, and "Vorwaerts" is the motto—we touch nowhere.

At Pola, the great Austro-Hungarian port and arsenal, we find six fine ironclads in harbour; they are in line, but have swung round so as to present the appearance of a perfect *echelon* to us as we steam along; forts innumerable crown every point. Pola has many Roman remains—not many Venetian; the amphitheatre held 20,000 spectators, and presents a very fine exterior, but the interior is a scene of desolation; the triumphal arch of the Sergii is very ornamental; there are two temples, and on Monte Zarro are several interesting remains, and the monument to Admiral Tegethoff, the hero of Lissa. Cap Promontore being passed, we turn north-eastwards, keeping the rich and beautiful coast of Istria in view, with Monte Maggiore in the distance. Abbazia, the Eden or "Paradies in nuce" of Austria, is crowded with fashionable visitors at this time; here is a "Quisisana" hotel among many others; the grounds of the Imperial Villa are lovely, and so are the fine promenades around; Abbazia is the gem of this Austrian Riviera, which is well protected from the scourge of the Adriatic, the dreaded "bora," and here, they consider, are combined the beauties of Cannes with its sweet flowers, of Sorrento with its oranges and citrons, and of Mentone with its scenery. From Abbazia to

KERKA FALLS.

Fiume is a fine sea walk of a few miles; here is the great Hungarian port; the whole bay is very beautiful, with its islands in front, and the snow-clad Dinaric Alps to the east.

CHAPTER II.

THE writer was favoured with real Italian weather throughout, and, proceeding one bright night through the Quarnerolo with its numerous islands, could realise—

> "Com' è gentil, un nott' in mezz' Avril,
> Azzur' il ciel, la lun' è senza vel "—

and, after passing the Puntadura an hour or two, a little miniature Venice appears in the distance: it is Zara, the capital of Dalmatia, glistening in the early sunshine—

> "She looks a sea Cybele, fresh from ocean."

ZARA.

[*To face page* 10.

On a peninsula, with her once strong battlements (now promenades), on which the old Lion of San Marco frequently appears, Zara is exquisitely situated, with the snow-clad Dinaric range to the north-east, and the island of Uglian opposite. The romanesque Duomo is interesting, and the Byzantine Church of San Simone has over its high altar the quaint Byzantine sarcophagus, containing the remains of the saint, whose bones wrought many miracles; there are some fine old Roman remains in the Giardino Publico—columns, etc. Venetian remains are seen on the walls of houses in every street. The town is, in common with all other towns under Austrian rule, perfectly clean; the people seem gentle and polite; picturesque costumes, Bosnian, Croatian, etc., are everywhere. The *inhabitants* all speak Italian, and do not like the *lingua tedesca*. Here is made the real maraschino from the *marasca* or wild cherry, which grows in profusion on the hills; they give you one kind with the cherries in it. Zara, founded by Augustus, for long was subject to Venice, but became so rebellious at the end of the twelfth century, that, finding "the domination of a monarch less insupportable than that of a republic," she gave herself up to the King of Hungary; this led to her being besieged in the Fifth Crusade, 1202, when her Cross, in which she trusted, failed to deter her Christian foes, and she was taken and pillaged by Venetians and French. From Zara to Sebenico is four to five hours by sea. Many islands and rocks with remains of old Venetian forts are passed. Sebenico is at the head of a bay entered by a narrow channel, at the entrance to which is Fort S. Nicolo,

THE WALLS OF DIOCLETIAN'S PALACE.

[*To face page* 12.

with a grand old Venetian lion. The town is very Venetian in style, with very narrow streets; the Duomo is Venetian Gothic, and has a very fine "Baptisterium"; the sculpture generally in the Duomo is most interesting. From the fort on the summit of Il Barone, one enjoys a splendid panorama. Near here is the River Kerka, on which a small steamer plies, and, having crossed the Lake of Proclian, we pass Scardona, and reach the celebrated Kerka Falls, which are highly picturesque and surrounded by fine, wild scenery.

> "Through sparkling spray, in thundering clash,
> The lightnings of the waters flash."

A few hours' sailing brings you to the quaint little town of Traü (the Tragurium of the Romans), on an island, connected by bridges with the mainland and also with the island of Bua. Traü is Venetian in style, and, strolling about, one comes across many exquisite little pieces of architecture. In the Duomo are many columns, especially those supporting the pulpit, with curious Byzantine capitals ; the sacristan displays many wonderful relics, vestments, etc., and a fine old illuminated book of 1289. From the summit of the graceful Campanile is a fine view ; a great expression of dismay came over the visage of the *custode* when I sounded *two* on the bell, it being about *four* o'clock. They have a great regard for time in these old-world places, where it is of little consequence, the clocks striking the whole hour, followed or preceded by the quarter, all through the day and night. Here, over an old gateway, a sturdy little evergreen is apparently springing out of the stone, and has been there for 300

THE CAMPANILE AT SPALATO.

[*To face page* 14.

years, shading and almost hiding the Lion of San Marco. It is a very pretty little excursion from here to the Bai Sette Castelli, and then to make the "giro" of the Bay with its seven little towns, beginning with Castel Nuovo; around this Bay is some of the richest land in Dalmatia. And now it is but two hours to Spalato, the principal object of everyone's journey in these parts; here is the wonderful Palace of Diocletian, eclipsed in size by the Escorial alone; here, near to his birthplace (either Salona or Dioclea), the wearied Emperor retired to spend his last years; within and *upon* the walls of this magnificent palace the old town is built, and these walls enclose an area of nine to ten acres. In the centre is the Imperial Mausoleum, now used as a Christian Duomo, and the model for the finest baptisteries; soaring above is the Campanile commenced in 1416; the interior of this temple is most impressive and beautiful, there is much scaffolding, etc., around, as many alterations are being most admirably conducted, and also removals, with a view to laying open this temple, the vestibule, and all the magnificent surroundings. The well-known archæologist, Monsignore Bulič, lives here, and it is a great pleasure to be accompanied round by such an enthusiast on the subject. During the performance of High Mass one morning in the *Settimana Santa*, no less than eleven common-looking fellows were up in the beautiful pulpit, leaning over, and scarcely adding to the effect contemplated by the architect. The museum contains much that is interesting, chiefly from the excavations at Salona.

Salona, a few miles inland, a once-buried

PORTA AUREA IN DIOCLETIAN'S PALACE.

[*To face page* 16.

city, must be visited with Monsignore Bulič. It was a celebrated Roman *seaport*, and was once the capital of Dalmatia, its amphitheatre, gateways, baths, and its walls testify to its ancient importance, its Christian cemetery contains many sarcophagi of interest. On a precipitous rock near Salona is the old fortress of Klissa. In Professor Freeman's " Cities Subject to Venice " is by far the best description of the wonders of Spalato, and of all these interesting places.

Still, " vorwaerts " is the word, and still our path lies o'er the sea ; one glorious night that we passed between the beautiful islands of Brazza, Lesina, Curzola, and many others, sky and water of the deepest blue, and, even after a fatiguing day, we lingered long on deck, enjoying the "rapture of repose" around :—

> " 'Twas sweet, when cloudless stars were bright,
> To view the wave of watery light,
> And hear its melody by night,"

and to think over that "shrine of the mighty" we had left behind at Spalato.

SPALATO. [*To face page* 18.

CHAPTER III.

AT Gravosa, where we arrive at daybreak, we take a small steamer up the river Ombla, and after about an hour and a half we arrive at the *commencement* (not the *source*) of the river; from underneath a perpendicular cliff of some 400 feet in height comes forth, in three rushes, the river, into a basin close under the cliff, of some 300 feet in depth and 180 across; then there is a weir-head, over which the water bounds, and is, at once, a fine broad river; it is supposed to be the same river that disappears under a mountain some thirty miles away. It is a natural wonder.

Beyond are the villa and grounds of Count Gozze; in these grounds are two splendid plane trees, said to be 1,000 years old; the larger one requires fifteen people with outstretched arms to encircle it. In a chapel here is a picture said to be by Titian. It is a pleasant excursion to the rich, park-like little island of Lacroma, where Cœur-de-Lion landed, and endowed the old Cathedral of Ragusa opposite, and where there is a handsome villa in the midst of a pretty garden. The island was the property of an Englishman, who built the villa and laid out the garden, and then drowned himself. It was afterwards a favourite retreat of the ill-fated Emperor Maximilian; it next belonged to Prince Rudolf, whose sad and

THE PERISTYLEUM, DIOCLETIAN'S PALACE.

[*To face page* 20.

mysterious end is still discussed; it is still imperial property, but the Emperor, considering that some evil agency must have prevailed, presented it to a religious body, and it is devoutly to be hoped that, by fasting, praying, dreaming, and carefully and religiously doing nothing, all that is satanic about it may be dispelled, and that, with the assistance of old Father Time, it may again become fit for an Arch-Duke's summer house. On the main land opposite is Ragusa, as Professor Freeman says, "The one spot on the Eastern Adriatic shore which never was subject to either Venice or the Turk." With its fine mediæval fortifications, we view Ragusa springing from the sea, more imposing by far than any other Dalmatian town, and with a natural rampart of hills at the back, and fortresses around; Ragusa has often shown her strength, and repulsed many an enemy. The town is quite Venetian in appearance, and has some handsome buildings; the chief is Il Palazzo Rettorale, a fine Renaissance structure, in which, upstairs, is a most interesting museum; it is Good Friday, the Procession of the Host is passing, and the people seem very devout. Southwards from Ragusa runs as beautiful a Riviera as Europe can show, indented with little inlets, banks covered with evergreens and spring flowers; this continues round the Bai Breno to Ragusa Vecchia, and we visit one of those curious *vrelli* (the term applied by the Italians to those streams springing suddenly from underneath the cliff or mountain); this one is utilised to work the Molino at Breno, and runs through a very picturesque nook in the

THE AMPHITHEATRE AT SALONA

[*To face page* 22.

bay. In harbour at Gravosa the ever kind and courteous Commandante of the *Metkovich* had arranged, one lovely evening, for a dance on deck, and—there being many young and charming Viennese ladies travelling—it was looked forward to with pleasure; the ship with its excellent lighting and brilliant display of bunting, with flags of all nations, looked its gayest; suddenly it was discovered that the gruesome season of Lent was not quite over—it was the last night—and devout people on shore might be shocked; general disappointment prevailed, and wishes were expressed that the inhabitants of small towns would not be so bigoted!

There is a small town in the most devout country in Europe, not far north of Mountserrat, where every respectable little " dawg " wears a black crape bow on his tail during Lent, and where all the animals, including the gentle "porco," to his great astonishment and inconvenience, are compelled to be religious, and to observe Good Friday by rigid fasting! As an admirable *set off* to this, however, in the renowned Zaragoza, there is always held, on Easter Sunday, *as duly announced*, a "*gran Corrida de Toros*," when six bulls are slaughtered, and a dozen horses turned inside out, in honour of Maria Santissima!

ENTRANCE TO THE MAUSOLEUM SPALĀTO.

[*To face page* 24.

CHAPTER IV.

ONCE more upon the sea,—

> "That tideless sea
> Which changeless, rolls eternally"—

and at sunrise it is truly beautiful as you enter the Bocca di Cattaro, leading to the finest inlet of the Adriatic, which forms what I have heard a naval officer describe as the "grandest harbour in Europe"; through several *bocche* you pass, and soon, facing you, is the once strongly fortified town of Castelnuovo, then several other towns, then through the narrow passage of *Le Cattene*, and then you emerge into what appears a lovely inland lake with two islands in the middle, and soon Cattăro is seen, with its fortifications running zigzag up the hill, and the mountains of Montenegro crowning all; the forts around are all of Venetian origin. The place was taken by the English from the French in 1813 and the whole garrison made prisoners. After a *giro* round this beautiful inlet, an ascent into Montenegro by the "wundervollen Serpentinenstrasse" (as the German guide-book calls the ascent) is of the greatest interest; after a drive of about five hours zigzag up the mountain, passing several forts, especially the strong Fort Gorazza, and enjoying magnificent views over the *bocche*, we cross the frontier into Montenegro, and another hour or so brings us to Njeguš,* in the midst of what has

* The sign "ᵛ" softens *s* into *sh*.

RAGUSA.

[*To face page* 26.

once been a lake; here, at an elevation of
4,000 feet, we are indeed in the heart of
the Black Mountains, after which the country is named. It is wild in the extreme,
huge rocks appear to have been hurled
everywhere, and houses and patches of
vegetation occupy the intervals. It is
Easter Sunday, and we see all the population *en fête*, with their national dances,
showing their delight that the gruesome
season is over; there are several open
stone circular enclosures in which the
"*Kolo*" is danced—a circle is formed, men
forming one-half, girls the other; two girls
and two men come to the front, dancing a
sort of wild jumping quadrille for about
three minutes, displaying great agility, then
each man kisses a girl, and they take their
places, to be followed by a similar quartette, and so on. A little farther on brings

us to Krivaško Schrjelo, rather more elevated; here is a scene of the very wildest desolation, as though chaos had come again; the cold is intense, ice and snow all around. We glance at the mountains of Albania and the great Lake of Scutari, and then are pleased to find ourselves descending, and, passing a few habitations, we wonder how life is there sustained. A thousand feet of "serpentinenstrasse," and we are at Cettinje, the capital of Montenegro, which has been likened to a Dartmoor village. One thing greatly impresses me, and that is the fine, soldier-like bearing of the handsome men; they and the boys all either salute or raise their caps; they are tall, active, and muscular, and in their Greek jackets and vests of various colours, Turkish knickers, either jackboots or stockings with a gold lace welt down the back, kam-

CATTARO (AT THE FOOT OF THE BLACK MOUNTAINS).

[*To face page* 28.

merband with daggers and pistols, and a small cap, worn like a 5th Lancer's, they look a fighting race,—they are, too. In the last encounter with their hereditary enemies the Turks, the Prince had explained to a fine old warrior who numbered more than eighty summers that he was too old to serve, and must remain behind,—hurt and insulted, the old man drew his revolver and blew his brains out. In the arsenal are several Krupp guns, all well kept, and a large collection of old Turkish weapons; there is also a fine old Venetian Lion resting in the Piazza—a trophy, I presume. Next day a long descent to Cattăro, and departure northwards. In the morning we arrive at the little island of Busi, far out in the Adriatic, and there visit the Dalmatian *Grott' azzura*. It has a loftier entrance than its sister at Capri, which it does not quite equal, although the various shades of blue are exquisitely beautiful, contrasting with the pitch darkness above.

Thence to the island of Lissa, and walk across from Comisa to Lissa (the capital). The island is fertile, and produces good wines. The English held it for three years. Near the mouth of the harbour of Lissa is a monument to the English Admiral Hoste, who defeated here a French fleet under Dubordieu, in 1811; above, on the hill, is Fort Wellington. Near is the island of Lesina (the "Corfu" of Dalmatia, to which all these islands belong); it is celebrated for its healthy and delicious climate; here are several Lions of San Marco. On what might be called the Acropolis of the town, is the fine Fort Spanuola, entirely Venetian, and commanding, from its battlements, a splendid view over the little Spalmadori

LA CROMA.

[*To face page* 30.

Islands, which form a breakwater in front of the harbour. On the many islands and rocks we pass after leaving Lesina, we see ruins of old Venetian forts, each telling its story of the past. It is worth while to go a few miles up the Fiume Narenta as far as Metkovič. It is the port for Herzegovina, and Mostar (the capital) is only two hours' distance by rail. A walk from Metkovič is the little town of Gaběla with its fort built by the Venetians. The Herzegovines are mostly Turkish in religion and habits. The men all wear the fez, and sit about *à la Turque;* the women all wear trousers, and an ungainly looking tunic and kammerband. They are an unsightly people compared with those we have left. Alas! northwards we are bound, and must say "Addio" to these sunny climes, where—

> "Long delighted
> The traveller fain would linger on his way."

We touch at Lussin, a charming island, in which is the busy little port of Lussin Piccolo (the next favourite Austrian health resort after Abazzia). It is a delightful walk to the romantically situated little town of Lussin grande. Lussin is very civilised, and teems with olive gardens and flowers.

And now, as we are nearing Trieste, I would pay a farewell tribute of praise to my fellow-travellers,—to the general excellent spirit of good-fellowship, and *camaraderie* prevailing,—to the beauty, elegance, and many graces of the Viennese young ladies, who are right in thinking this Dalmatian trip a "safe" one,—to the kindness, courtesy, and gallantry of the Captain and officers of the good ship *Metkovitch*, which delightful qualities seem

LUSSIN GRANDE, IN THE ISLAND OF LUSSIN.

[*To face page* 32.

especially characteristic of the Austrian people. And to any lover of the old Venetian story, who may have been led to follow these interesting old footprints, I would suggest, as a charming route thence to England, to proceed *viâ* Adelsberg, Graz, Vienna (for as long a stay as he can), Nürnberg, Frankfurt and the Rhine, and would hope that he may have escaped the " Allgemeine cabine," and the " Bora."

LA CROMA.   [*To face page* 34.

II.
EASTWARDS.

IN MEMORY OF 1866,
AND OF THE
LATE LAMENTED LADY,
WHO CAUGHT THE SHARK.

R.I.P.

(*i.e.*, NOT THE SHARK, BUT THE L.L.L.)

EASTWARDS.

"PA! whereabouts is the Valley of Diamonds?" was the question once propounded by a youthful Hebrew to the sagacious author of her being.

"The Walley of Diamonds! that depends on the *shize* of 'em, my dear," was the cautious reply, which probably did not quite satisfy the inquiring young spirit.

Oh! gentle reader, alas! we cannot promise to take you even in imagination to this particular valley—you yourself will be the only *real* gem throughout. Still our journey will be across seas of the brightest emerald and of the richest and deepest sapphire, even through *vallies*, for weeks together, of the purest waters. Yes, would you see nature in her most varied moods, and, at the same time, court health, novelty, and life-long memories—time being of no consequence to you—make up a pleasant party, select a good "taut" sailing ship, a *tight* ship, but with a *sober* crew, and, *à propos* of gems, you may embark at worse places than Kingstown, in—

"The Emerald Isle, that gem
Set in the imperial diadem"—

for Calcutta.

Such was the writer's fate; it was, in fact, his honeymoon; but happy though it was, it involved changing the sweet island of the pig, the Pat, the pratie, and the one-pound note, for the land of the punkah, the pariah, the pagoda tree, and the wily rupee. The sadness of farewell is felt at these times ; so the good ship bounded away, one form remained conspicuous on the pier, and although seen through a vista of years, the vision of that bright particular star will ever remain sharply engraven on the retina of the writer's eye—'twas no less than his mother-in-law!

"Ah! memory, fond memory!
When all else fails, we turn to thee."

'Twas one July, the beautiful bay and the Wicklow hills soon faded from our view. We soon experienced all the tossing, heaving, lurching, and rolling that a *lively* ship is capable of. After tacking about for a month we crossed the line, and were becalmed for some days in the *doldrums*; we afterwards continued far south-west until, about 50 miles from Rio, we met with favourable breezes, which carried us down far south of the Cape, even to 40° south latitude; and then, after two months from home, we met with those wonderful rollers from Cape Horn, on which, with a strong wind, we were wafted eastward; *here* were the vallies of the purest waters; from the crest of one wave to that of the next was more than a quarter of a mile, and it was far more sensational than any switch-back or wheel at Earl's Court. Some people on hearing of these waves seem inclined to take it all with *a grain* of salt—we took it with *many*, even salt junk for a change! We encountered a severe gale in these tremendous seas, and, for three days and nights, were all fastened below. During this terrible time, it appeared from facts afterwards brought to light, that the soldiers, having discovered that we were taking out a cargo of beer, had very carefully removed some planks enclosing the cargo, and drowned their cares. Happily, our crew was composed of young Scotchmen, for whom the beer had not a similar temptation, but—

> " Had ta mixture peen,
> Only half Glenlivat,"—

this veracious account might not have been written!

The gale having abated, the chief amusement was catching sharks, and the unfortunate albatrosses. One fine morning a lady was watching a bait in the shape of a huge piece of pork attached to a cable, over the stern of the ship; it so happened that an enormous shark, accompanied, as usual, by a little pilot-fish, was eyeing it—

"Look there," said the shark, "if that isn't a fine piece of pork, I'm a sardine."

"Beware!" said the pilot-fish; "I see something like a hook projecting from it, and God never made a porker like that."

"Porker, be ——," said the voracious one, and swallowed the bait.

"Well, there you are then, stoopid! hooked! or I'm a grampus!" said the loquacious pilot-fish; "so now I'll hook it myself—ta-ta!"

The lady was the sole witness as to this *finny* conversation, and, of course, claimed to have caught the monster, which was sixteen feet in length, and took eighteen men to haul it on deck, where its antics became dangerous—one lash of its tail shook the vessel—whereupon, a sailor deftly gave it a *coup de grâce* with a chopper, breaking its spine. It proved to be a female, and, as she was viviparously inclined, four baby sharks were prematurely ushered into the world. They were next reintroduced to one another in a tub of water, and became very hilarious, and soon indulged in a free fight. What remained of them after this was made into a curry by the sailors, who found it a pleasing change from salt junk. A *post-mortem* was duly held on the shark, and, very carefully stowed away in a corner was found a Tommy Atkins's jacket—a search was made for the Tommy, but it was surmised that he had executed a strategical movement, and retired; thus finishes the *tail* of a shark!

It was nearly three months now since we had seen land, and one morning it was pleasing to hear the dulcet voice of the captain of the maintop proclaiming that Amsterdam Island was in sight, and we turned northwards for the Bay of Bengal. One afternoon we counted more than twenty whales gambolling together, and trying which could blow the highest ; their babies were all looking on approvingly, and the spectacle would have gladdened the heart of that old connoisseur, Polonius.

A commander of one of these transport ships is very restricted as regards the punishment he may award to any member of his crew for any breach of dicipline,— our Captain's ultimatum was to strike a man off duty, knowing that his comrades would make his life a burthen to him. As an instance, one fine day a young sailor thought he would commence to beguile the tedium of a tropical afternoon by bestowing a kiss upon the tempting and ruby lips of the young wife of a corporal, who, in his wrath, *went* for that amorous child of the ocean. A disturbance ensued, and, as the sailor was afterwards very insubordinate, the Captain inflicted what he told me was the severest punishment he could award,—he struck the man off all duty for a week. On about the fourth day the sailor came begging to be allowed to return to duty. But said the Captain,—

"Na, yer'll no do yer-r duty till yer-r holiday's expired, and ah hope yer-r enjoying it."

Never shall we forget those wonderful sunsets every evening in the Bay of Bengal, far surpassing even those of Egypt in their colouring and infinite variety. It was the middle of October, just the commencement of the hurricane season. A little north of the latitude of Madras we were becalmed. A tremendous sea arose, without a breath of wind, and continued for three days and nights. The yards of the good ship touched the water every roll; everything breakable on board was smashed. This fearful sea had been raised by a hurricane which had passed some sixty miles astern of us. After this we proceeded northwards till we saw the low-lying country about the delta of the Ganges,—the first land since leaving Kingstown, four months before. At last, arrangements were made with a pilot, and after about 100 miles up the Hoogly, we found ourselves at Calcutta. This was not, however, our destination; but, after a month spent in Barrackpore, we journeyed up country to Meerut, and, oh! reader of inquiring mind, the end of October is just the time to commence exploring all these

LUCKNOW.

[*To face page* 46.

places of extremest interest—Meerut, Delhi, Cawnpore, Agra, Lucknow, Benares, etc.

You will, perhaps, have escorted your *carrisima sposa* to the gorgeous East, and may deem it advisable to take a bungalow, say, at Lucknow. In this case you will rejoice in your *fourteen* domestics, Hindoos and Mussulmans, and will be able to study their peculiar idiosyncrasies. They are excellent in many ways, and although you live with doors and windows open for months together, you may live for years in India without losing a thing. Should you suffer at all from torpidity of the liver, it is probable that, by a process of gentle but continued irritation, in which being materially assisted by mosquitoes, white ants, etc., they may serve as a corrective, you will doubtless acquire, under the guidance of the gentle Munshi, a little colloquial

Hindustani. You will soon discover that the Mem Sahib is far more able to control your establishment than you are. In your endeavours to get your wishes carried out it is possible that the sweetness of your temper may be occasionally tried. We have known men, *wise* men of philosophical turn of mind, men who were rarely given to using even a great big D, so sorely tried that, at last, livid with wrath, and well-nigh demented with fury, they have let out with arms, legs, and boots, in all directions, thundering volleys of vituperation, such as only *this*, the most *flowery* language on earth, is capable of, using terms terrible enough, if translated, to have made the corpses of their great grandfathers wriggle in their graves, or have brought a blush to the cheek of a costermonger's donkey!

THE DHUL CANAL, KASHMIR.

[*To face page* 48.

The mild Hindoo, as also the Mussulman, thinks that language was given him to conceal his thoughts, and, as with that "Heathen Chinee," or as we are just now experiencing in our dealings with the Turks respecting Armenia, their ways are *peculiar*.

At a court-martial assembled not far from Lucknow, the writer, being a member, noted down the following scraps of cross-examination, which may show slightly that it is difficult to get much out of an ordinary native in the way of truthful evidence:—

Q.—Do you know the prisoner?

A.—I am a poor man, and would not tell a lie.

Q.—Do you recognise the prisoner?

A.—I know him by his marks.

Q.—What marks?

A.—Two moles on his face.

Q.—Can you see the moles on his face?
(*Prisoner was in a very bad light, with his back to it.*)

A.—No, *Gharib-purwur* (protector of the poor).

Q.—Then how can you say you recognise him?

A.—(*In a high key.*) *Gharib-purwur!* I am a poor man; how can I presume to know!

. . . .

Q.—When you last saw the prisoner, was he alone?

A.—No, he was with two *Sowars*, and a *ghora* led by a man.

Q.—Are you quite sure that the man was not being led by the *ghora*?

A.—If your honour says so, I will swear it. I am a poor man.

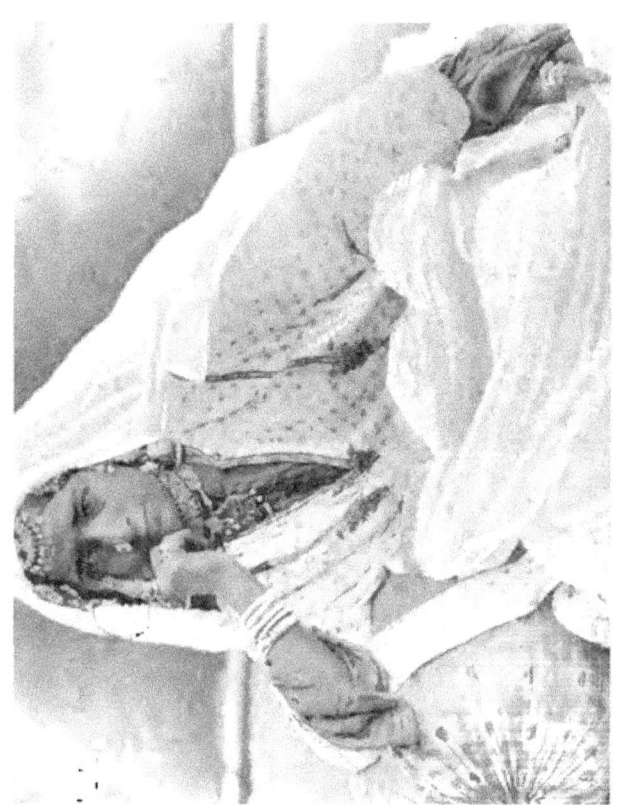

Q.—At what distance was he when you saw him?

A.—About 700 yards off.

Q.—How was he dressed?

A.—In a pair of shoes and a *puggree*.

Q.—Had he nothing else on?

A.—*Gharib-purwur*, he was far away, and it was a dark morning.

Q.—You have a long sight; how far can you see?

A.—As far as I can distinguish.

Q.—But how far can you distinguish?

A.—May I be blown from a gun if I would tell a lie—I cannot, being a poor man, distinguish further than I can see.

The prisoner afterwards, in his defence, confronted the above witness with a policeman.

Q.—(*to K* 22) Would you believe that man upon his oath?

A.—No.

Q.—For what reason?

A.—Because, although he is the son of only one mother, I know he has had a hundred fathers! (*Sensation in Court.*)

The prisoner was honourably acquitted. It is possible that it is probable (a favourite expression with the Bengali Baboo) that by the end of April, having explored and enjoyed all those above-named interesting places, and having confessed to yourself that Europe contains nothing so beautiful, so impressive, as that most exquisite " Dream in Marble," the Taj Mahál, you may begin to think the plains of Bengal are getting rather warm—in fact, that you have had a taste of the hot weather. You are no exception, all the world and his wife are thinking the same; but, as they cannot *all* go to the hills, very often it

happens that duty compels "all the world" to remain grilling in the plains below, whilst his *placens uxor* goes off to Kashmir, Simla, Mussourie, Nynee Tal, etc., and still contrives to enjoy herself! You have, being your own master, an *embarras de richesses* indeed before you, viz., all from Kashmir to Darjeeling. You may now enter Kashmir with great facility, and will be richly repaid by enjoying the whole summer in that "Valley of bliss," fair as this earth can show, 5,500 feet above the sea,—

"With its roses, the sweetest that earth ever gave,
 Its temples, and grottoes, and fountains as clear
 As the *love*-lighted eyes that hang over their wave."

They *do* tell me that *love* is now assisted by *lucre*, at a tariff fixed by the paternal Hindoo Government, which duly exacts a percentage! Perhaps your Lucknow friends may allure you to Nynee Tal, which, of course, is much more easily reached, and which has many charms peculiarly its own. From it you should visit Almorah, and if you desire sport, and are bent on a venturesome excursion, you should procure at Almorah a *hushiyár* (clever) Khansamah—a man who can prepare you a good dinner at any time, anywhere, *with* nothing and *out of* nothing, and at the same time look after your tent and Coolies (the writer was favoured with a prodigy of this kind)—and go to the Pindari Glacier. It will take you a fortnight, and you will have to rough it, and to cross many nerve-trying places by rope bridges, and even by a single rope, if you follow the route by the river. The summit of the glacier is about 15,000 feet, but, arrived there, you see towering above

THE PINDARI GLACIER.

[*To face page* 55.

you into the blue ether the magnificent *Nunda Devi*, 27,500 feet, on which the glacier, where the Pindar River has its source, is situated. You may return by another route, far safer, but infinitely less wild and picturesque.

The "leave season" is over on October 15th, and shortly before that a stampede to the plains commences. Of course *you* will take it leisurely, and whether you afterwards spend a month or two at Calcutta or at Bombay, previously to your return, we think you will agree that for a change of life and habits, for beautiful climate (*i.e.*, for one who is his own master), for novel experiences of all sorts, it would be difficult to suggest anything more enjoyable than sixteen months in India.

III.

THE EVIL EYE·
OR,
THE COLONEL IN QUEST OF HIS REGIMENT.

TO
THE MARCHESA DI TESTAFERRATA,
IN
MEMORY OF A PILGRIMAGE.

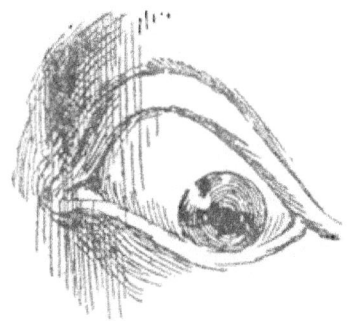

THE EVIL EYE;
OR,
THE COLONEL IN QUEST OF HIS REGIMENT.

"There's a divinity that shapes our ends, rough-hew them how we will."—*Hamlet.*

MOST of us who lead active lives find, at times, our intentions thwarted and our plans frustrated, in ways utterly unforeseen, just as they appear on the eve of fulfilment; we find the mysterious *force majeure* dominating sometimes our wills and actions, so that we suddenly become the creatures of the strangest circumstances, and meet with, perhaps, the most curious adventures of our lives.

In the year of grace '85 I was in command of my battalion at Fort Ricasoli, Malta; in May of that year I proceeded on five months' leave of absence to England. After the delights of London, I was enjoying a few days of *dolce far niente* late in August, in a romantic spot in the Isle of Wight, when I received a telegram ordering me immediately to rejoin my battalion, as it was to embark on the 11th September for the Straits Settlements. Having studied the matter, I determined to proceed *viâ* Calais, Lucerne, the St. Gothard, Rome, and Naples, then by steamer, so as to arrive at Malta in good time; this seemed a perfectly happy arrangement.

I may mention *en passant* that I was perfectly aware of the cholera prevailing at times in Spain and even Marseilles, but as the news from Italy stated that *ottima salute* (the best of health) prevailed there, I laughed at the warning of a prophetic friend—" I know you will be quarantined," and started by the above route. As light-hearted as was the oft-quoted Ollivier, and as confident as one can be of anything mundane, was I, whilst wafted southwards, that I should arrive in time; at Genoa, Milan, the papers all proclaimed the *ottima salute* throughout Italy; at Rome, to my horror, I read that Sicily had instituted five days' quarantine for all arrivals from Italy! My steamer was to touch there, and I should never reach Malta in time! At Naples I ascertained that another steamer would leave three days later, *direttamente* for Malta. This was cheering; it was duly announced in the papers. This would serve me; the

Gods appeared propitious, and I one of the elect!

Naples, in September, is a warm but not a sweet place; the Hotel de Genéve (where I put up, as it was near the quays and *bureaux*) is not what I should recommend to the fastidious. It is certainly cheerful, it noise can make it so, and there are mosquitoes and other lively provisions of nature for "preventing the human liver becoming torpid." Anxiously, with my heart in my mouth, and not putting too much faith in the *bureau d'aministrazione*, I was longing for the day fixed for departure, when, on calling one morning at the *bureau*, I was informed that there would be no communication with Malta except *viâ* Sicily, with its five days' quarantine. *Corpo di Bacco!*—what did it mean? That I could not reach Malta till the 15th. However, I felt conscious of having done all in my power to rejoin in time, and confident that I could prove it on arrival in Malta, and then take a passage for the East. I could now do nothing but endeavour to preserve my sanity, study the environment, accept the inevitable, and make the most of it. Awaiting embarkation in that good ship *Sumatra* was almost maddening. The day arrived; for distraction I attended in the morning High Mass at the Cathedral of San Gennaro (it was the day of the purification of the Virgin), and then went on board. I found the first mate on deck in a paroxysm of rage, with his gold-lace cap thrown down, shaking his fists towards the heavens, and abusing the Virgin terribly. I supposed that something had gone wrong with him at Mass, but soon discovered the cause of this expense of energy to be, that so much merchandise had to be stowed, that the ship could not start at the appointed time; it was pleasing to meet a man with a soul for punctuality! Shortly afterwards a notice appeared that, in consequence of a *forza maggiore*, our departure would be postponed till next day.

During the evening great crowds assembled on shore to give vent to their feelings at the Sicilians having established quarantine. They said it was groundless, and simply in retaliation for the quarantine in Italy the previous year; the ways of the cholera microbe are certainly inscrutable, and it would seem that the authorities in Sicily are under the impression that the insinuating bacillus reserves himself for a sea voyage, as not a single case had occurred on shore.

At last we started for Sicily; it was a glorious day, and the lovely bay looked its best, the only cloud visible was the smoke resting above Vesuvius. Our passengers were a heterogeneous collection; of course, we had many Sicilians homeward bound, some for Palermo, not knowing how they were illustrating the old *incidit in Scyllam*, etc. We had a man in search of his wife,—he said he had left her a few weeks ago at Messina in charge of his money-bags, but had heard she had left, and had gone either to Constantinople *viâ* Genoa, or to Paris *viâ* Algiers! He was a trustful man, and seemed very happy! We had a plump and fair *prima donna* for Catania, and a lean and dark one for Palermo; an ex-German officer, turned wine-merchant, who had lost his nose at Gravelotte; a few Sisters of Mercy; some

Italian officers and men joining their regiments quartered in Sicily; and lastly, eight British subjects, of whom I was one (and the only Englishman on board), bound for *il fior del mondo*, as the Maltese lovingly call their sea-girt home.

At 9 a.m. the following day we touched at Reggio, there to hear that cholera had broken out at Palermo; this meant that there would be no escape from Sicily, as a Sicilian epidemic sets the whole Mediterranean in a panic. In the evening we dropped anchor in the Bay of Augusta (a few miles north of Syracuse), where, after a palaver, our papers were handed to the health officers through the medium of a pair of tongs; they then came on board, and we all marched past in slow time before them for inspection, after which four elderly but robust Sicilians, with broad glaring yellow and red sashes, were placed over us as our *garde sanitaire*, and we entered on our five days' quarantine.

Next day (11th) was the date fixed for the regiment's departure, and I, the colonel, virtually a prisoner, was separated from it by only seven hours' journey! Was this Nemesis?

We had a pleasant little *table d'hôte* on deck, under the awning, which for dinner was removed, and we sat *sous la belle étoile;* we eight for Malta soon became acquainted, and exchanged mutual condolences; having studied Italian for some months in Malta, I was too glad to have such an opportunity of improving myself. On hearing of my repeated disappointments, my companions at once said that it was clear that a *mal occhio* (evil eye) was upon me, that I was under a *jettatura* (a something cast, a spell), that the malignance was palpable, and a lady told me that I ought to pray to the Virgin night and day that it might be averted.

It is a pleasure to look back on having here made the acquaintance of Colonel the Count Dal V—— bound for Palermo, where he was chief of the staff; he is a most accomplished officer, and good companion; he thought well of the Sicilian soldiers, and told me that they and the Piedmontese are the best soldiers in the Italian army; those on board were five young fellows of good physique.

We were strictly looked after by the *garde sanitaire* to see if any of us showed signs of illness, or any desire to escape; they were a comical quartette, and we named them San Domenico (the patron saint of Augusta), San Pietro, Don Pasquale, and

Don Giovanni, and sometimes a funny man would throw something overboard after dark, so as to make a splash in the water, when it was refreshing to see the excitement among the *garde sanitaire,* who always thought some passenger was trying to elude their vigilance.

Very soon the news arrived that at Malta fourteen days' quarantine in separate rooms at the *Lazaretto* was the order for all arrivals from Sicily. Now this was piling Vesuvius on Etna—Pelion on Ossa was nothing to it! Oh! thought I, for a Newgate cell! Shades of Pestal and Bonnivard! this was the crowning sorrow, verily a *jettatura maladetta* pursued me! I tried to write to my friends, but my pen refused,—I wrote to *Vanity Fair* instead. I sought consolation alternately in laughing at the *garde sanitaire,* and in reflecting that *l'uomo propone, il dio dispone*, and *che sara sara*.

Having completed five days *in contumacia*, as they call it, we landed and radiated off, —we eight hurried to Syracuse; of course, we clung to the idea that possibly we might still be allowed across, on showing that we had not been near any infected port.

The epidemic raged at Palermo, and hundreds a day were dying; the population, frenzied with alarm, believed that the germs of cholera were being spread by agents of the Italian Government to thin the population, particularly among the poor. We found all Syracuse in a wild state of panic; new arrivals were in danger, and everywhere looked on with suspicion: a *cordon* was formed every evening to prevent all chances of refugees coming in from Palermo, and if one walked outside the city gates one had to take a sort of return ticket. In Syracuse, as in every town in Sicily, the ignorance and disregard of the commonest laws of sanitation are appalling; the whole town is one vast temple of Cloacina, and everything is done to invite cholera ; there is nothing a Sicilian loves so much as a stench, and little groups collect so as to discuss politics, family matters, or the cholera news, usually selecting for the purpose one of the many unsavoury corners in every street, terrace, or piazza.

In the midst of these fervent worshippers of the goddess aforesaid, with almost tropical heat, with mosquitoes all day and night, and with the prospect, if any cholera showed itself, of having our throats cut, or being otherwise disposed of, we lived in hopes; it is probable, however, that the good Sicilian wine helped to sustain us.

It is a great pleasure to recall to mind the kindness and hospitality of Madame and Mademoiselle B., the charming wife and daughter of the acting British Consul, who was away ill at the time; it was at their suggestion that, after a few days, I drew up a formal petition to the Governor of Malta, which we all signed, asking that we might be allowed across, even to the Lazaretto.

While waiting for His Excellency's decision to arrive, there was time to explore and enjoy the many objects of interest in and near Syracuse. The best walk in the neighbourhood is to the ancient fortress of Epipolæ, the stronghold of Dionysius; it is said to be the best preserved specimen of Greek military architecture to be seen anywhere; the rock out of which it is cut is perfectly adamantine, and there is nothing about it to tempt the curio-hunting, nose-chipping tourist; would that the grand *temples* of antiquity had been so unmolested.

One day, strolling alone among the mighty dead in the labyrinthine *catacombi*, I was wondering how many of those countless thousands had attained—

"Nirvana where the silence lives"—

or whether, with restless craving, they all were still enduring, still struggling on, in different states of being; suddenly I stumbled, and my candle went out; after much groping about it was a great pleasure to find myself in the sunshine once more.

Hidden in a wild and weird hollow, far

from human habitations, is the celebrated "Ear of Dionysius," up in which the tyrant used to sit concealed so that he might listen to the conversation of his captives far below. Driving out one afternoon with two friends to visit this extraordinary acoustic contrivance, we had left the high road, and preparatory to plunging into the jungle path leading to the wonderful *orecchio*, our Jehu thought it the correct thing to descend and kneel, crossing himself before a little shrine with a figure of the Virgin; he then drove on, and in about five minutes, when crossing a rather rough and rutty piece of ground, one of his fore-wheels came off, whereupon he again descended, livid with wrath and shaking his fist at the sky, poured forth a fearful torrent of abuse, addressed to the gentle *madre di dio*, to whom he even applied an epithet

THE EAR OF DIONYSIUS.

[*To face page* 74.

almost rhyming with *gitana!* What a simple faith was his, almost on a par with that of the Mandingo or Fantee of West Africa, who throws away or smashes his fetish when anything goes wrong.

The favourite promenade at Syracuse is by the sea, leading to the flowery and shady nook in the gardens, where is the statue of the great defender of Syracuse, the sage Archimedes; and here is the fountain of Arethusa, the nymph who

". . . . . . Arose
From her couch of snows,
In the Acroceraunian mountains,"

and, transformed into a fountain, vanished underground in Eblis, to reappear—

"In Enna's mountains,
Down one vale were the morning basks;"

here she ripples past a murmuring stream-
let, which the gold-fish love, till she takes
her final plunge

"Under the ocean foam."

CHAPTER II.

A week had elapsed since I wrote to Malta, when a letter arrived, saying that His Excellency could not sanction our crossing to Malta; it was now clear that we must look about for some other means of escaping from Sicily. I saw, in the paper, mention of an English steamer lying at Catania, and bound for Trieste. To Catania, then, we went, and had an interview with the captain of the steamer, but he said he had strict orders, by telegram from home, to take no passengers whatever, for any sum of money, from Sicily. At Catania we found that no Italian port would receive us, unless we previously underwent two weeks' quarantine off Asinara, in the north of Sardinia. A young English artillery officer whom I met, and who was on three months' leave from India, had just arrived, and had arranged to endeavour to join his family at Como *viâ* Asinara; I hope he obtained an extension of leave!

Catania is, perhaps, the finest and most attractive town in Sicily (Palermo being the most picturesque); its public gardens are particularly pretty and well laid out; situated near the foot of Etna, it has suffered terribly at times from lava torrents, but the worst catastrophe that ever befell it was the earthquake in 1693, when 18,000 inhabitants perished. Etna was far from quiescent when we were there, flames or burning lava being frequently emitted; on this stupendous volcano, 11,000 feet in height and ninety-one miles in circumference, there are, despite its 700 cones and *bocche*, sixty-three towns and villages, and 300,000 inhabitants—of such value are the ashes for the cultivation of the vine. From here comes the good Sicilian wine, exported to many ports in such enormous quantities (50,000 pipes from Marsala alone), and so valued at Bordeaux for assisting the oft-failing vintages, in allowing itself in disguise to do duty as St. Julien, St. Estephe, St. Emilion, etc.

Underneath the Duomo are the remains of an old Greek temple of Bacchus. The supply of water for the baths in the temple ran down from a considerable height on Etna; in an eruption about 300 B.C., the lava flowed down the watercourse, and has solidified in huge adamantine masses in the temple. It is possible that it might be well if baths and cleanliness of habits in general were nowadays encouraged by the priesthood among their flocks, whose conduct in life is so much influenced by their spiritual pastors. I have already alluded to the pestilence-inviting ways of the people as regards their out-door practices, but find it more difficult to comprehend what there is in the beautiful and spirit-cleansing adoration of Santa Maria, Santa Agata, etc., to necessitate the disgusting habit of spitting about in the cathedrals and churches. I recollect once, when wrapt in admiration at the magnificent proportions of the interior of St. Peter's from near the south-west corner, being driven as far as the left transept, in my anxiety to place distance between me and a sacrilegious devotee, voiding his rheum in front of Michel Angelo's Pieta! Did the ancients thus defile the temples of their

gods? Would a Jew have thus desecrated the temple of Solomon? Would a Roman or Greek have thus polluted the shrines of Apollo or Athene? It has always appeared to me that the priests might with advantage remind or instruct the people that cleanliness is next to godliness, and thus more favourably impress the mind of the enquiring traveller, who is apt at present to leave these lovely regions of the sunny south with the conviction that, judging by the outward and visible signs, the Christianity prevailing has a distinctly *cloacinaic* tinge about it.

After remaining four days here we considered it advisable to proceed to Messina; all plans had been discussed, even that of waiting at Aci Reale or Taormina, until cholera had abated; there seemed no better plan, so to Messina we went.

At Messina I ascertained that, although there was no chance of getting a passage, as I so much desired, to any port farther east, I could in about a week proceed to Marseilles and thence by the *Messageries Maritimes* to Singapore; this idea of Marseilles recommended itself also to my companions. We all agreed that it was of no use to be down-hearted, and were quite a pleasant little society among ourselves; we acted on the good principle, *dum vivimus vivamus*, and enjoyed ourselves; the bright and cheering sunshine cast on us by the sweet presence of the Marchesa di T—— and Madame M., who with their husbands and three other Italian gentlemen, formed with myself the party, infused an atmosphere of life and gaiety, and we were anything but gloomy. I have most agreeable recollections of a charming little party of pleasure organised by the Marchesa to the picturesque and romantic shooting-box of her brother, the Prince di Sta. M——, a few miles drive from Messina; the Prince was away at Palermo heroically risking his life, and alleviating the awful misery in the cholera-smitten town; the King, who is invariably foremost where real pluck and courage are required, had expressed his intention to visit Palermo, with the view of encouraging and inspiring the populace by his presence, but was happily dissuaded. Much kindness and courtesy were shown us by the British Consul, who had seen and travelled much. I recollect his telling me that on the first news of the outbreak of the epidemic at Palermo, he had ordered out from London several dozen bottles of some strong disinfectant, intending to give it to the poor round about the Consulate; but he had taken the advice of a friend, who had told him it would be dangerous to do so, as he would be at once suspected of spreading cholera among them. So rooted was this fancy among the poor that, in Palermo, many people had been shot or stabbed for having been seen holding a handkerchief with camphor to their noses in passing some foul, malodorous quarter; it was even unsafe to be seen entering a chemist's shop!

On a fine evening in October we bade adieu to Trinacria; looking across the beautiful Straits we seemed tantalisingly near to the Calabrian shore, about four miles distant; the sun set soon afterwards in a blaze of glory; everything promised well; before retiring for the night we sighted the Lipari Isles, and passed close under the ever-active Stromboli. The next day we were able to see Garibaldi's house on Caprera, then through the Straits of Buonafacio, after which we had a glimpse of the entrance to Ajaccio; a gentle breeze made us dance a little; by the third day we were encountering a strong maestrale, against which we did not do much—for our small steamer it was a gale; it was perhaps partly in deference to the wishes of our party that our *Commandante* altered our course, so that we rounded Cape Corso with a view to getting under lee of the land of Corsica; for the first day we certainly derived some advantage, but the next day a strong scirocco arose and blew steadily, at the same time that the maestrale prevailed on the west side of the island; the ladies, and in fact most of our party, were much alarmed. I do not think they had been on a rough sea before; we had not a very large supply of provisions on board, and after beating backwards and forwards (some twenty miles) for two days and nights, we sent a boat to the small town of Macinaggio to buy some provisions; the inhabitants, however, turned out *en masse*, and threatened to fire on us and our boat if we did not depart. The gale on the west side being stronger than ever, we went down the coast; we had now been a week or more at sea; the scirocco increased to half a gale, the weather was *burrascoso*, the demeanour of the inhabitants seemed hostile to us, our provisions were running short, the look-out was not promising; there was much fear and terror on board, and much bead-telling and cries, repeated in all keys, of "*Santa Maria! madre de Dio! prega per noi!*"

One day we had been discussing the

situation; we had some sardines, some *finocchio*, and some casks of prickly pears, and we recollected having that morning heard chanticleer proclaim the break of day,—*gioja!* our live stock was not exhausted! We all went forward to inspect; we discovered, residing up near the forecastle, one elderly feathered biped who for years had paced the deck and weathered many a *burrasca;* his harem had all vanished one by one; things looked ominous, and he was making a sumptuous but solitary meal, as though in prescience of his coming doom,—perhaps it was in thoughtful consideration for us, or perhaps he reflected that, as had before happened, his harem might be renewed, and his joys recommence. We regarded him somewhat carnivorously; he contemplated us with a wistful, enquiring look in his starboard eye; our earnest gaze seemed to shatter his hopes. Yes! thought he, his time was approaching, and soon he would be sent to follow those loved and lost ones; but how would his gallinaceous spirit have been consoled, and what visions of glory have burst upon his chanticlerical imagination, could he have foreseen that the feathers adorning his posterior would ere long be paraded in pomp and circumstance, waving in the helmet of some gallant *bersagliere!* We besought our accomplished *chef* to carefully carry out his final injunctions as to whether he preferred to be roasted or boiled, and —we left him.

A happy thought struck a French wine merchant on board, who entertained hopes of one day getting to Bordeaux, that he had a friend in the Syndic of Bastia (the second town in Corsica); it was determined

BASTIA.   [*To face page* 88.

to proceed thither, and to submit that, eight or nine days having elapsed since we had left Sicily, we might be allowed to land. The oracle was worked, we eight paid the harbour dues, and, never since that eventful day in the annals of the human race, when the ark rested on Ararat, did a party of eight souls set foot on *terra firma* with greater delight than we did; that night we dined and slept at the Hotel de France, Bastia. Here, then, ended another little fytte of my pilgrimage. By this time the regiment had arrived at Singapore; the distance between it and me seemed to be steadily increasing; was I to regain it in this century or the next, and reappear a species of military Rip Van Winkle? When was the drama to end? What was to be the *dénouement?* There were nine days to wait for the regular

French steamer to Marseilles; the weather was too bad to tempt the *mistral* in the Gulf of Lyons on the *vaporino* by which we had arrived.

There is much sound philosophy in the French saying, "Quand on n'a pas ce qu'on aime, il faut aimer ce qu'on a;" we acted up to that, and life at Bastia seemed to us, by contrast, very pleasant. Bastia is the second town in Corsica, and of some commercial importance; it is surrounded by picturesque scenery; seawards, to the east, were visible Elba, Capraia, and Monte Cristo's Isle; the people, of course, are far more Italian than French, although they generally profess Republican principles. There is a leading man in Corsica who is looked on as a very pronounced Republican, but wears a gold coin, struck for Napoleon IVth, next his heart! Who can wonder at a Corsican having Napoleonic fancies? There was a fine French regiment here, the 138me; many more like it will be required before *la révanche* takes place.

The Corsicans think highly, and rightly so, of their fine chalybeate spring at Orezza, in the mountains; the water has more acid and iron in it than any other, and our acting Consul told me that a small tumbler of it in the morning was the finest tonic; we drank it at the hotel *ad lib.*; it was sold in Corsica for 3 sous a bottle, but throughout France it fetched 1½ francs.

It was with great delight that we embarked for Marseilles; the *mistral* had moderated slightly, we had a larger steamer, and, after rather more tossing about than the ladies found agreeable, arrived the evening of the following day off the Isle of the Chateau d'If; shortly afterwards we passed a vigorous medical inspection, and were allowed to land. That same evening, on enquiring at the bureau, I was informed,— *sacrebleu! sapristi! ventre sain gris!*—that the *Messageries Maritimes* packet for the East had left on the previous day! I really think that even St. Lazarus, who fled thither after having been raised, and became the first patron Saint of Marseilles, would have used strong language at this! The next steamer would not leave for a fortnight; my friends opined that the *jettatura* had not yet been averted from me, and I was invited to accompany La Marchesa the next morning on a little pilgrimage to Notre Dame de la Garde; high on a pinnacle is the little church so highly venerated by all who have narrowly escaped the perils especially of the deep; it commands a grand sea-view over the blue

NÔTRE DAME DE LA GARDE.

[*To face page 92.*

water. Little tapers were carried by us up the ascent and duly placed on the altar; the music, the sweet voices, the spirit-soothing calm of the place crept o'er me, and,—they who choose may take it *con grano sali*,—induced a conviction that by the combined influences of the sweet blue eyes of the Madonna, and the bright flashing orbs of the handsome *Marchesa*, the malign effects of the *mal occhio* were at last averted, and that the next move would lead to my goal.

The stream of life flows very agreeably at Marseilles; the climate in October is lightful; the *Cannebiére* is ever gay and lively; the hotels and cafés are good. One may indeed rest and be thankful in that charming verandah of the Hotel Rubian, admiring the glorious sea-view and enjoying the most delicious *bouillabaisse* in France.

After a few days our little party divided;

the two married couples took a villa on the Prado, intending to remain there till the cholera had died out, then to travel by land to Reggio, and cross thence to *il fior del mondo*, that "gem set in a silver sea"; they were not anxious again to tempt the rolling deep; they preferred to contemplate it from their island home, and were sated with the joys to be found upon its heaving bosom. In their society many hours of my two months' agony had been most agreeably beguiled, and,—recollecting their complimentary and pleasing wishes *a rivederla* on parting,—I find myself regretting that past friendship should ever come to be regarded as one of *les illusions perdues!*

The time soon arrived for my departure in the magnificent steamer *Anadir* for the far East. Prince Jerome Bonaparte came on board to see his son, Prince Louis, comfortably cabined, as he was starting on a trip round the world; many French consuls for India, Burmah, China, came with many belongings to see them off; several charming young Dutch ladies, married and single, bound for Java; some Irish girls, sisters of the Society of "Le bon Pasteur," with some elderly sisters in charge, for Ceylon; Dutch officers for Sumatra, &c.; a Japanese minister and his family; all these and many others were arranged for, and then—

"Adieu! sweet land of France, adieu!"

we steamed off. A gentle breeze was with us the whole length of the Mediterranean to Port Said, but we did not use the sails, as these crews do not much approve of canvas, and sometimes flatly refuse to raise it. The ships of the *M.M.* are well appointed and fitted up in every way, the most perfect order and regularity prevail, the cuisine is excellent, and the table most liberally kept. I would allude to the trustworthiness of the cabin attendants. Many a time on entering my cabin after morning chocolate I have found money, which I had carelessly left about, placed conspicuously in the middle of my berth, so that I must see it. It would appear that a different system prevails as regards *treasure trove* in certain ships on which we are wafted to and fro! The navigation on board the *M.M.* is worked with great precision; such precaution is taken to avoid the faintest suspicion of laxity, that the officers never join in any dancing or other amusements.

I like the sociability on a French ship which admits of intercourse between the different classes, if they desire it, and as most of our young ladies were in the *Pays Bas*, as they patriotically called their part of the ship, they came and were welcomed to all our dances, which were frequent, and kept up with spirit. One of the sisters bound for Ceylon was a lovely girl, and of a high type of beauty, and such as one pictures when reading—

"The light of love, the purity of grace
 The mind, the music breathing in her face;"
. . . .

hers was a face that Sodoma or Andrea del Sarto would have immortalised; at those hours when conversation was permitted her, she loved to talk of Ireland and the home she had left for ever; at times she was full of Irish fun and humour; she was the admiration of all, and was invariably called *La Madonne de Ceylon*. All honour to those sweet sisters; their devotion and the good they do are incalculable. Still, on those bright mornings in the Red Sea, at hour set apart for meditation, I have watched her angelic face, her blue eyes rigidly fixed on the deck as though nothing less than a messenger from heaven descending in a water-spout could raise them, and blamed the fates that such a *chef d'œuvre* of nature should be thus sacrificed, and breathe nought but the odour of sanctity; it might be that a messenger *would* one day arrive in the form of—

"*L'Amour, qui fait l'aurore enchantée de toute existence,*"

and come to the rescue, and change the current of her life. Then when one remembered the *société* to which she belonged, there was the melancholy reflection that it was possible, if not probable, that perhaps l'Amour—improving some holy occasion, and embracing the tempting opportunity,—might come masquerading in the gruesome garb of some seductive *bon pasteur!*

The Prince was most courteous and agreeable; he speaks English perfectly; *écarté a quartre* with him, his A.D.C. and a Mons. S. (bound for Saigon) beguiled the hours in the afternoon. H.H. left us at Aden to await the Bombay steamer, as he intended to spend three months in India. We had a fine passage across the Indian Ocean, and I realised, with feelings of much pleasure, that I was now at last approaching home (the Regiment) at the rate of 300 miles a day; a short stoppage at Colombo, and then four days found us in the Straits of Malacca with its wonderful current. Some Dutch engineer officers on board had some very elaborate plans relating to the fearful volcanic eruption of Krakatoa in August, 1883; it, perhaps, was felt over a wider area than any other in the history of man. One-half of the island subsided to an unfathomable depth; a tidal wave was caused 100 feet in height, which destroyed, in a few minutes, the town of Angers in Java, with 17,000 inhabitants, and carried on its crest a steamer for nine miles into the interior of Java; the sound of the eruption was heard at Ceylon and even farther, and ashes from it fell in showers at Singapore; the whole earth's atmosphere was affected by it for some time after. We were rapidly nearing the equator, the heat was great and suggestive of a vapour bath. All said that it was a very healthy time of year, as the north-east monsoon (the *maestrale* here)

SINGAPORE. [*To face page* 100.

had just set in. The approach to Singapore is picturesque, and there is much richness in the vegetation around; cocoanut, nutmeg, every kind of tropical fruit tree abounds; it is the land of the delicious mangosteen. On the afternoon of the 28th November we arrived. As I stepped on shore, a weight, a burden, seemed to fall off me. I wondered if Ulysses (*parvis componere magna*), that weary wanderer, when, after having escaped Scylla and Charybdis, he had gained the ever-fragrant bowers of Calypso's isle; or even if Jonah, when he found himself ejected, after his three days' discomfort (I had had three months), felt greater joy than I did.

I found a sympathetic letter awaiting me from that kind friend and excellent soldier, now departed, who was then commanding the troops in Malta; and, thanks to the

General in the China command, the whole of my expenses from Marseilles were afterwards granted me. Right proud have I been for thirty years to be associated with the British soldier; but never did I behold one with greater delight than the first time after landing, when I beheld a red coat of the Buffs.

IV.

THE EXPECTED BUDDHA;
OR,
THE ROYAL TWINS.

TO
THE SPIRIT OF DISTRACTION,
WHICH LED THE WRITER TO SIAM,—AND IN
GRUESOME MEMORY OF
DECEMBER 10TH, 1886.

THE EXPECTED BUDDHA;

OR,

THE ROYAL TWINS.

CHAPTER I.

One December, a few years ago, the writer embarked at Singapore for Bangkok, the Capital of Siam. The north-east monsoon was prevailing, and, after bounding for four days over those magnificent rollers coming down from the China seas, and, having passed the "Pulo Panjang" and two other rocks in the Gulf of Siam, the mighty

Meinam (the Mother of Waters) was entered; shortly after appeared Fort Puknam, on the left bank, and soon Bangkok, the so-called "Venice of the Far East," was seen in the distance. As we approached, we were struck with the semi-Venetian look of the place, with its numerous canals, and its immense rafts of linked bamboos, on which are streets of substantial houses and shops. On the canals and creeks around are seen many floating islets of houses: thousands of Siamese are said never to have set foot on land. On landing, the most pretentious modern building seen is the Royal Seminary; but the lofty Buddhist Temples or "Wats" give the character to the place. The hotels are, of course, very primitive; but the writer had the good fortune to be invited to stay at the British Legation, there to meet with the kindness

BANGKOK. [*To face page* 105.

The Expected Buddha.

and splendid hospitality of the Consul, who is now our Minister in Japan. To one who had been living for a year in Malaya, in a sudorific state, the climate here seemed, at this season, delightful, the nights being cool and pleasant. Bangkok is a densely populated city of 350,000 inhabitants of all Oriental nationalities. The industries are mostly carried on by Chinese, as the Siamese are not a very industrious race. They are rather a mean, and certainly not a highly-favoured people by nature. The women wear their hair quite short, and do not contrast well with their handsome neighbours, the Burmese, with their laughing, sparkling eyes and rich wavy tresses; they are not too straight-laced in their morals, and, of course, a man may have as many wives as he likes, and he generally prefers them young. Their dress is simple, consisting of a "sarong" which is fixed round the waist, caught up between the legs gracefully, and hitched behind; boys and girls wear a top-knot of hair, which they twist into a lump, and when they reach puberty (about thirteen) this is cut off, and the hair allowed to grow all over the head.

At this time the Queen of Siam, who was the King's half-sister, was the happy mother of twins, of five months old. Shortly before their birth, the Siamese doctors declared that she was about to bring forth a white elephant, and the idea was supported by the priests, who affirmed that another Buddha was expected on earth (a Buddha *always* arrives in the form of a snow-white elephant), but the doctor of the British Legation, on being consulted, disillusionised them with, "No; not a white elephant, your Majesty—*only* twins!" Their

A CANAL AT BANGKOK.

[*To face page* 108.

birth was a great source of royal joy, as no Queen of Siam had ever had twins before. One of these twins died during my visit, and I witnessed the extraordinary funeral procession to the temple, where the body was to be cremated the following day. The procession was two miles in length, and included all the embodied Siamese Army, each regiment with its band, and many elephants bearing palanquins containing gold-coloured priestly robes presented by the King to the various temples. The hearse was a species of pagoda, with sixteen long silver cords pendant from the corners, each held by a Siamese on foot, in European evening dress and tall hat with crêpe streamers. The hearse was followed by a *swarm* of 400 nuns in gold-coloured raiment (that being the sacred colour), and, with their heads closely shaven, they resembled a sea of cocoa-nuts, going along, all were chattering or wailing—verily a sight for the gods! The King, borne aloft on a golden palanquin by many subjects, concluded the procession. The Queen and women of the Court proceeded by a different and far shorter route to the temple, and long curtains or purdahs were held by female police, with a view to screening them from the public gaze. After a few days, I was presented to, and most courteously received by, His Majesty. We (the Consul and I) were ushered into the royal presence by the King's half-brother, who has visited England, and talks English well. The audience hall is very handsome, and the arms of Siam (the elephant with three trunks) was very noticeable. The King was looking over a large illustrated work on

INTERIOR OF ROYAL TEMPLE.

[*To face page* 110.

Rome. He was then thirty-three years of age, and smart and intelligent. He moved about as an active man is supposed to, and there was nothing of luxurious, lazy Orientalism about him. He had just received a splendid orchestrion from Paris, which was placed in the hall of the palace, and interested him greatly. His Majesty is very enlightened, and busies himself much in all that relates to the welfare and improvement of his country and people. He has travelled in India, and was pleased to converse about it, and to find that I recollected his visit, some years before, to Benares. The Royal Temple ("Prakas Wat") is very ornate. In it is the celebrated Emerald Buddha, a figure eighteen inches high. It is placed twenty-five feet from the ground over a kind of altar, and is said by some to be of crystal, by others of jade; but certainly the eyes are two magnificent emeralds. The white elephants are disappointing, as they are *not* white. About their ears and some other parts some patches of a dirty cream colour are to be seen. They are undersized, and very dirty, even to their tusks, and although they are each one tenanted by the soul or consciousness of a departed prince, they do not greatly impress one who has been for many years admiring the fine, stately animals to be seen in India.

The temples in Bangkok are interesting. In "Wat Poh" is the great *reclining* Buddha, 150 feet in length, covered throughout with pure gold. At "Wat Saket" the dead are all cremated, except those who are unable to pay for it; and these are cast to the birds of the air. I saw a corpse

WAT CHANG (TEMPLE OF THE ELEPHANT).

laid out, with six vultures sitting expectant on a branch above; but, I believe they were disappointed of their banquet, as this corpse was for cremation. The Temple of the Elephant ("Wat Chang") is the finest of all, it is 189 feet high, and commands a fine view all around.

Priests are very numerous. There is a law compelling all young men on reaching the age of twenty-one to join the priesthood for one year, during which they have to lead correct and even ascetic lives, and if caught departing from the paths of virtue lose their heads! After this they have to give three months every year to military training. There is much trade in slaves, in Siam, and in Cambogia and Annam many males and females are sold—a Cambogian fetching 250 tikàls, an Annamite 100; a tikàl is sixty cents.

The Siamese *permanent* army is less than 4,000, officered largely by Danes, but with English words of command and drill, and English dress. If required 30,000 men might be available. The King had some gatling guns, three batteries of small brass cannon, and two of small Armstrongs. Some of the infantry are armed with Martini-Henrys, and the majority with Snyders. The Siamese are not a fighting race, and certainly do not look so. The city (proper) is surrounded by a wall (with rampart) 17 feet high. There is a fort (Fort Puknam) with some guns on the left bank of the Meinam, near which is a pagoda.

Ever since the French expedition in 1866, to explore the country between Cochin China and Yunnam, the Siamese have been uneasy and distrustful of French intrigue. They have lately, in their answers

ENTRANCE TO WAT CHANG.

to the French demands, shown up to the world the absurdities of the French in expecting Siam to cede territory which did not belong to her. This perhaps is not wonderful, when the Gallic ignorance of geography is considered; but it is remarkable that a country which has so signally failed, whenever it has attempted to colonise, should lecture *us* on the subject of *états tampons* or buffer states.

www.ingramcontent.com/pod-product-compliance
Lightning Source LLC
Chambersburg PA
CBHW020846160426
43192CB00007B/804